Great Works Instructional Guides for Literature

Henry and Mudge: The First Book

Based on the book by Cynthia Rylant
Great Works Author: Jennifer Lynn Prior

Image Credits
Andrew Mitchell (cover; page 11); Timothy J. Bradley (pages 61–62); All other images Shutterstock

Standards
© 2007 Teachers of English to Speakers of Other Languages, Inc. (TESOL)
© 2007 Board of Regents of the University of Wisconsin System. World-Class Instructional Design and Assessment (WIDA)
© Copyright 2010. National Governors Association Center for Best Practices and Council of Chief State School Officers. All rights reserved.

Shell Education
5301 Oceanus Drive
Huntington Beach, CA 92649-1030
http://www.shelleducation.com
ISBN 978-1-4258-8959-3
© 2014 Shell Educational Publishing, Inc.

The classroom teacher may reproduce copies of materials in this book for classroom use only. The reproduction of any part for an entire school or school system is strictly prohibited. No part of this publication may be transmitted, stored, or recorded in any form without written permission from the publisher.

Table of Contents

How to Use This Literature Guide 4
   Theme Thoughts 4
   Vocabulary 5
   Analyzing the Literature 6
   Reader Response 6
   Guided Close Reading 6
   Making Connections 7
   Language Learning 7
   Story Elements 7
   Culminating Activity 8
   Comprehension Assessment 8
   Response to Literature 8

Correlation to the Standards 8
   Purpose and Intent of Standards 8
   How to Find Standards Correlations 8
   Standards Correlation Chart 9
   TESOL and WIDA Standards 10

About the Author—Cynthia Rylant 11
   Possible Texts for Text Comparisons 11

Book Summary of *Henry and Mudge: The First Book* 12
   Cross-Curricular Connection 12
   Possible Texts for Text Sets 12

Teacher Plans and Student Pages 13
   Pre-Reading Theme Thoughts 13
   Section 1: Henry Gets a Dog 14
   Section 2: Henry Walks to School 23
   Section 3: Mudge in Henry's Room 32
   Section 4: Mudge Gets Lost 41
   Section 5: Henry and Mudge Back Together 50

Post-Reading Activities 59
   Post-Reading Theme Thoughts 59
   Culminating Activity: Reader's Theater 60
   Comprehension Assessment 64
   Response to Literature: Benefits of Owning a Pet 66

Writing Paper 69

Answer Key 71

Introduction

How to Use This Literature Guide

Today's standards demand rigor and relevance in the reading of complex texts. The units in this series guide teachers in a rich and deep exploration of worthwhile works of literature for classroom study. The most rigorous instruction can also be interesting and engaging!

Many current strategies for effective literacy instruction have been incorporated into these instructional guides for literature. Throughout the units, text-dependent questions are used to determine comprehension of the book as well as student interpretation of the vocabulary words. The books chosen for the series are complex and are exemplars of carefully crafted works of literature. Close reading is used throughout the units to guide students toward revisiting the text and using textual evidence to respond to prompts orally and in writing. Students must analyze the story elements in multiple assignments for each section of the book. All of these strategies work together to rigorously guide students through their study of literature.

The next few pages describe how to use this guide for a purposeful and meaningful literature study. Each section of this guide is set up in the same way to make it easier for you to implement the instruction in your classroom.

Theme Thoughts

The great works of literature used throughout this series have important themes that have been relevant to people for many years. Many of the themes will be discussed during the various sections of this instructional guide. However, it would also benefit students to have independent time to think about the key themes of the book.

Before students begin reading, have them complete the *Pre-Reading Theme Thoughts* (page 13). This graphic organizer will allow students to think about the themes outside the context of the story. They'll have the opportunity to evaluate statements based on important themes and defend their opinions. Be sure to keep students' papers for comparison to the *Post-Reading Theme Thoughts* (page 59). This graphic organizer is similar to the pre-reading activity. However, this time, students will be answering the questions from the point of view of one of the characters in the book. They have to think about how the character would feel about each statement and defend their thoughts. To conclude the activity, have students compare what they thought about the themes before the book to what the characters discovered during the story.

How to Use This Literature Guide (cont.)

Vocabulary

Each teacher reference vocabulary overview page has definitions and sentences about how key vocabulary words are used in the section. These words should be introduced and discussed with students. Students will use these words in different activities throughout the book.

On some of the vocabulary student pages, students are asked to answer text-related questions about vocabulary words from the sections. The following question stems will help you create your own vocabulary questions if you'd like to extend the discussion.

- How does this word describe _____'s character?
- How does this word connect to the problem in this story?
- How does this word help you understand the setting?
- Tell me how this word connects to the main idea of this story.
- What visual pictures does this word bring to your mind?
- Why do you think the author used this word?

At times, you may find that more work with the words will help students understand their meanings and importance. These quick vocabulary activities are a good way to further study the words.

- Students can play vocabulary concentration. Make one set of cards that has the words on them and another set with the definitions. Then, have students lay them out on the table and play concentration. The goal of the game is to match vocabulary words with their definitions. For early readers or English language learners, the two sets of cards could be the words and pictures of the words.

- Students can create word journal entries about the words. Students choose words they think are important and then describe why they think each word is important within the book. Early readers or English language learners could instead draw pictures about the words in a journal.

- Students can create puppets and use them to act out the vocabulary words from the stories. Students may also enjoy telling their own character-driven stories using vocabulary words from the original stories.

Introduction

How to Use This Literature Guide (cont.)

Analyzing the Literature

After you have read each section with students, hold a small-group or whole-class discussion. Provided on the teacher reference page for each section are leveled questions. The questions are written at two levels of complexity to allow you to decide which questions best meet the needs of your students. The Level 1 questions are typically less abstract than the Level 2 questions. These questions are focused on the various story elements, such as character, setting, and plot. Be sure to add further questions as your students discuss what they've read. For each question, a few key points are provided for your reference as you discuss the book with students.

Reader Response

In today's classrooms, there are often great readers who are below average writers. So much time and energy is spent in classrooms getting students to read on grade level that little time is left to focus on writing skills. To help teachers include more writing in their daily literacy instruction, each section of this guide has a literature-based reader response prompt. Each of the three genres of writing is used in the reader responses within this guide: narrative, informative/explanatory, and opinion. Before students write, you may want to allow them time to draw pictures related to the topic. Book-themed writing paper is provided on pages 69–70 if your students need more space to write.

Guided Close Reading

Within each section of this guide, it is suggested that you closely reread a portion of the text with your students. Page numbers are given, but since some versions of the books may have different page numbers, the sections to be reread are described by location as well. After rereading the section, there are a few text-dependent questions to be answered by students. Working space has been provided to help students prepare for the group discussion. They should record their thoughts and ideas on the activity page and refer to it during your discussion. Rather than just taking notes, you may want to require students to write complete responses to the questions before discussing them with you.

Encourage students to read one question at a time and then go back to the text and discover the answer. Work with students to ensure that they use the text to determine their answers rather than making unsupported inferences. Suggested answers are provided in the answer key.

How to Use This Literature Guide (cont.)

Guided Close Reading (cont.)

The generic open-ended stems below can be used to write your own text-dependent questions if you would like to give students more practice.

- What words in the story support . . . ?
- What text helps you understand . . . ?
- Use the book to tell why _____ happens.
- Based on the events in the story, . . . ?
- Show me the part in the text that supports . . . .
- Use the text to tell why . . . .

Making Connections

The activities in this section help students make cross-curricular connections to mathematics, science, social studies, fine arts, or other curricular areas. These activities require higher-order thinking skills from students but also allow for creative thinking.

Language Learning

A special section has been set aside to connect the literature to language conventions. Through these activities, students will have opportunities to practice the conventions of standard English grammar, usage, capitalization, and punctuation.

Story Elements

It is important to spend time discussing what the common story elements are in literature. Understanding the characters, setting, plot, and theme can increase students' comprehension and appreciation of the story. If teachers begin discussing these elements in early childhood, students will more likely internalize the concepts and look for the elements in their independent reading. Another very important reason for focusing on the story elements is that students will be better writers if they think about how the stories they read are constructed.

In the story elements activities, students are asked to create work related to the characters, setting, or plot. Consider having students complete only one of these activities. If you give students a choice on this assignment, each student can decide to complete the activity that most appeals to him or her. Different intelligences are used so that the activities are diverse and interesting to all students.

Introduction

How to Use This Literature Guide (cont.)

Culminating Activity

At the end of this instructional guide is a creative culminating activity that allows students the opportunity to share what they've learned from reading the book. This activity is open ended so that students can push themselves to create their own great works within your language arts classroom.

Comprehension Assessment

The questions in this section require students to think about the book they've read as well as the words that were used in the book. Some questions are tied to quotations from the book to engage students and require them to think about the text as they answer the questions.

Response to Literature

Finally, students are asked to respond to the literature by drawing pictures and writing about the characters and stories. A suggested rubric is provided for teacher reference.

Correlation to the Standards

Shell Education is committed to producing educational materials that are research and standards based. As part of this effort, we have correlated all of our products to the academic standards of all 50 states, the District of Columbia, the Department of Defense Dependents Schools, and all Canadian provinces.

Purpose and Intent of Standards

Standards are designed to focus instruction and guide adoption of curricula. Standards are statements that describe the criteria necessary for students to meet specific academic goals. They define the knowledge, skills, and content students should acquire at each level. Standards are also used to develop standardized tests to evaluate students' academic progress. Teachers are required to demonstrate how their lessons meet standards. Standards are used in the development of all of our products, so educators can be assured they meet high academic standards.

How To Find Standards Correlations

To print a customized correlation report of this product for your state, visit our website at http://www.shelleducation.com and follow the online directions. If you require assistance in printing correlation reports, please contact our Customer Service Department at 1-877-777-3450.

Introduction

Correlation to the Standards (cont.)

Standards Correlation Chart

The lessons in this book were written to support the Common Core College and Career Readiness Anchor Standards. The following chart indicates which lessons address the anchor standards.

Common Core College and Career Readiness Anchor Standard	Section
CCSS.ELA-Literacy.CCRA.R.1—Read closely to determine what the text says explicitly and to make logical inferences from it; cite specific textual evidence when writing or speaking to support conclusions drawn from the text.	Analyzing the Literature Sections 1–5; Guided Close Reading Sections 1–5; Story Elements Sections 2–3
CCSS.ELA-Literacy.CCRA.R.2—Determine central ideas or themes of a text and analyze their development; summarize the key supporting details and ideas.	Analyzing the Literature Sections 1–5; Guided Close Reading Sections 1–5; Making Connections Sections 2, 4; Post-Reading Response to Literature
CCSS.ELA-Literacy.CCRA.R.3—Analyze how and why individuals, events, or ideas develop and interact over the course of a text.	Analyzing the Literature Sections 1–5; Guided Close Reading Sections 1–5; Story Elements Sections 4–5; Post-Reading Response to Literature
CCSS.ELA-Literacy.CCRA.R.4— Interpret words and phrases as they are used in a text, including determining technical, connotative, and figurative meanings, and analyze how specific word choices shape meaning or tone.	Vocabulary Sections 1–5; Analyzing the Literature Sections 1–5
CCSS.ELA-Literacy.CCRA.R.10—Read and comprehend complex literary and informational texts independently and proficiently.	Guided Close Reading Sections 1–5
CCSS.ELA-Literacy.CCRA.W.1—Write arguments to support claims in an analysis of substantive topics or texts using valid reasoning and relevant and sufficient evidence.	Reader Response Section 3
CCSS.ELA-Literacy.CCRA.W.2—Write informative/explanatory texts to examine and convey complex ideas and information clearly and accurately through the effective selection, organization, and analysis of content.	Reader Response Sections 1, 4
CCSS.ELA-Literacy.CCRA.W.3—Write narratives to develop real or imagined experiences or events using effective technique, well-chosen details and well-structured event sequences.	Reader Response Sections 2, 5; Story Elements Section 1

Introduction

Correlation to the Standards (cont.)

Standards Correlation Chart (cont.)

Common Core College and Career Readiness Anchor Standard	Section
CCSS.ELA-Literacy.CCRA.W.4—Produce clear and coherent writing in which the development, organization, and style are appropriate to task, purpose, and audience.	Reader Response Sections 1–5; Story Elements Sections 1–2, 4–5; Culminating Activity
CCSS.ELA-Literacy.CCRA.L.1—Demonstrate command of the conventions of standard English grammar and usage when writing or speaking.	Reader Response Sections 1–5; Language Learning Sections 1, 3–5; Story Elements Section 1; Making Connections Section 4
CCSS.ELA-Literacy.CCRA.L.2—Demonstrate command of the conventions of standard English capitalization, punctuation, and spelling when writing.	Language Learning Section 2
CCSS.ELA-Literacy.CCRA.L.4—Determine or clarify the meaning of unknown and multiple-meaning words and phrases by using context clues, analyzing meaningful word parts, and consulting general and specialized reference materials, as appropriate.	Vocabulary Sections 1–5
CCSS.ELA-Literacy.CCRA.L.6—Acquire and use accurately a range of general academic and domain-specific words and phrases sufficient for reading, writing, speaking, and listening at the college and career readiness level; demonstrate independence in gathering vocabulary knowledge when encountering an unknown term important to comprehension or expression.	Vocabulary Sections 1–5; Culminating Activity

TESOL and WIDA Standards

The lessons in this book promote English language development for English language learners. The following TESOL and WIDA English Language Development Standards are addressed through the activities in this book:

- **Standard 1:** English language learners communicate for social and instructional purposes within the school setting.
- **Standard 2:** English language learners communicate information, ideas and concepts necessary for academic success in the content area of language arts.

Introduction

About the Author—Cynthia Rylant

Cynthia Rylant grew up in West Virginia. At one point, she lived with her grandparents in the mountains. They had no electricity or running water. This life with her grandparents was her inspiration for writing *When I Was Young in the Mountains*. She writes of taking baths in the kitchen, using an outhouse, and spending time with family. Many of her books are about her life growing up.

She started writing children's books after she took an English class in college and hasn't stopped since. She loves cats and dogs and writes about many of her pets from over the years in her books. *Cat Heaven* features Edward Velvetpaws and Tomato, two of her beloved kittens.

While children of all ages love Cynthia Rylant's books, the Henry and Mudge books rise to the top as favorites for young children. The series describes the adventures of a young boy named Henry and his huge dog and loving companion, Mudge.

More information about Cynthia Rylant and her books can be found at the following website:

- http://www.cynthiarylant.com

Possible Texts for Text Comparisons

There are about 30 Henry and Mudge books in the series. A few memorable titles include: *Henry and Mudge in Puddle Trouble*, *Henry and Mudge and the Tall Tree House*, *Henry and Mudge and the Forever Sea*, and *Henry and Mudge and the Snowman Plan*. These books can be used as comparisons to *Henry and Mudge: The First Book*.

Introduction

Book Summary of *Henry and Mudge: The First Book*

Cynthia Rylant writes a story of love and companionship between a boy and his dog. This book contains seven short chapters about Henry and Mudge. Henry wants a friend to play with and his parents get him a dog. Mudge is a huge dog that loves Henry and makes him feel safe and loved. When Mudge gets lost, Henry searches for him and brings him home. Henry and Mudge do not want to be separated ever again.

Cross-Curricular Connection

This book can be used to explore social studies concepts, such as responsibility, friendship, companionship, and pet ownership.

Possible Texts for Text Sets

- Carney, Elizabeth. *National Geographic Readers: Cats vs. Dogs.* National Geographic Children's Books, 2011.
- Newman, Aline Alexander and Gary Weitzman. *How to Speak Dog: A Guide to Decoding Dog Language.* National Geographic Children's Books, 2013.
- Osborne, Mary Pope. *Magic Tree House Fact Tracker #24: Dog Heroes: A Nonfiction Companion to Magic Tree House #46: Dogs in the Dead of Night.* Random House Books for Young Readers, 2011.
- Spears, James. *National Geographic Kids Everything Pets: Furry Facts, Photos, and Fun—Unleashed!* National Geographic Children's Books, 2013.

or

- Day, Alexandra. *Good Dog, Carl.* Aladdin Paperbacks, 1997.
- MacLachlan, Patricia. *Waiting for the Magic.* Atheneum Books for Young Readers, 2012.
- Willems, Mo. *Pigeon Wants a Puppy.* Disney-Hyperion, 2008.

Name _____ Date _____

Introduction

Pre-Reading Theme Thoughts

Directions: Draw a picture of a happy face or a sad face. Your face should show how you feel about each statement. Then, use words to say what you think about each statement.

Statement	How Do You Feel? 😊 ☹️	Explain Your Answer
Dogs make great friends.		
Being alone can be scary.		
It is sad to lose a pet.		
It is not important to have a close friend.		

Teacher Plans—Section 1

Henry Gets a Dog (pages 5–13)

Vocabulary Overview

Key words and phrases from this section are provided below with definitions and sentences about how the words are used in the story. Introduce and discuss these important vocabulary words with students. If you think these words or other words in the story warrant more time devoted to them, there are suggestions in the introduction for other vocabulary activities (page 5).

Word	Definition	Sentence about Text
brothers (pg. 5)	male siblings	Henry wishes he had a **brother**.
sisters (pg. 5)	female siblings	Henry does not have a **sister**.
friends (pg. 5)	companions; people to spend time with	Henry wants to have **friends**.
street (pg. 5)	a road in a city or town that has houses or other buildings on one or both sides	Henry has no friends on his **street**.
children (pg. 7)	more than one child	No **children** live on Henry's street.
floppy (pg. 10)	soft and flexible	Mudge has **floppy** ears.
collars (pg. 11)	harnesses that fit around the neck	Mudge grows out of seven **collars**.
one hundred eighty pounds (pg. 12)	an amount of weight	Mudge weighs **one hundred eighty pounds**.
drooled (pg. 12)	dripped out of the mouth	Mudge **drools** on Henry.
licked (pg. 13)	covered with a tongue	Mudge **licks** Henry's face.

Name _____ Date _____

Pages 5-13

Vocabulary Activity

Directions: Choose at least two words from the story. Draw a picture that shows what these words mean. Label your picture.

Words from the Story

brothers	sisters	friends	street	children
floppy	one hundred eighty pounds	drooled	licked	collar

Directions: Answer this question.

1. Henry wants **friends**. How is having a dog like having a **friend**?

_____

_____

Teacher Plans—Section 1

Henry Gets a Dog (pages 5–13)

Analyzing the Literature

Provided below are discussion questions you can use in small groups, with the whole class, or for written assignments. Each question is written at two levels so you can choose the right question for each group of students. For each question, a few key points are provided for your reference as you discuss the book with students.

Story Element	Level 1	Level 2	Key Discussion Points
Character	Why does Henry want a dog?	What changes Henry's parents' minds about getting a dog?	Henry is lonely because he is an only child and there are no children who live on his street. He asks for a dog and his parents almost say no, but they realize that a dog would be a good friend for Henry.
Character	How does Mudge change as he grows?	What kinds of things does Mudge outgrow and why?	Mudge starts out small as a puppy, but he grows to be a very large dog. He keeps outgrowing his collars and his cages, so the family has to keep buying larger ones for him.
Plot	Describe the kind of dog Henry wants.	In what ways is Mudge the perfect dog for Henry?	Henry does not want a dog with pointed ears or curly hair. Mudge loves Henry, licks him, and sits on him.

Name _____ Date _____

Pages 5-13

Reader Response

Think

Think about something that you have seen grow. It could be a flower, a garden vegetable, a pet, or a baby.

Informative/Explanatory Writing Prompt

Write about something that you have seen grow. Describe the different changes that happened as it grew.

_____
_____
_____
_____
_____
_____
_____
_____
_____
_____
_____

Pages 5-13

Name _____ Date _____

Guided Close Reading

Closely reread about Mudge as a puppy (pages 9–13).

Directions: Think about these questions. In the space below, write ideas or draw pictures as you think. Be ready to share your answers.

❶ What reason does Henry give for Mudge being so short at first?

❷ Which text from these pages shows that Mudge likes Henry a lot?

❸ What does Henry say to his parents that shows he is happy they allowed him to get a dog?

Name _____ Date _____

Pages 5-13

Making Connections—Owning a Pet

Owning a pet is a big responsibility. That means you have to make good choices for your pet. Read about being a good pet owner.

- **Space**—A good pet owner thinks about where a pet will live. A large dog needs a yard or a place to walk.

- **Food and Supplies**—Different pets need different kinds of food. A large dog eats a lot of food. A dog needs a leash and a collar. A cat needs a litter box. All pets need water to drink.

- **Time**—Some pets need more time than others. A fish does not need a lot of time. A dog or a cat needs an owner who will spend time with the animal. They need to play and be loved.

- **Health Care**—All pets need special care to be healthy. Dogs and cats need regular visits to a veterinarian for shots and medicine.

Directions: Under each type of pet, write the needs it has. You can use each need for more than one animal.

Pet Needs

food	leash	toys
water	love	litterbox

Dog   **Cat**

_____   _____

_____   _____

_____   _____

_____   _____

Pages 5–13

Name _____ Date _____

Language Learning–Count the Syllables

Directions: All of the words below are from this section of the story. Read each of the words to yourself. If the word contains two syllables, circle it.

Language Hints!

- Every syllable has just one vowel sound.
- Words with suffixes are divided between the root word and the suffix.

had   brother   parents   friends

Henry   different   sorry

collars   almost   dog   pets

because   said   home   looked

then   children   face   okay

hug   short   curly   ears   one

pointed   Mudge   floppy   fur

puppy   growing   cage   seven

street   live

Name _____ Date _____

Pages 5-13

Story Elements–Character

Directions: Henry does not want a short dog. He does not want a curly dog. He does not want a dog with pointy ears. Draw a picture of a dog that Henry would like. Do not draw Mudge.

Pages 5-13

Name _____ Date _____

Story Elements–Plot

Directions: Henry wants someone to play with. He finally convinces his parents to let him have a dog. Pretend you are Henry. Write a letter telling all the reasons why you should get to have a dog.

_____,

_____

_____

_____

_____

_____

_____

_____

_____

_____

                                                 _____,

Teacher Plans—Section 2

Henry Walks to School (pages 14–17)

Vocabulary Overview

Key words and phrases from this section are provided below with definitions and sentences about how the words are used in the story. Introduce and discuss these important vocabulary words with students. If you think these words or other words in the story warrant more time devoted to them, there are suggestions in the introduction for other vocabulary activities (page 5).

Word or Phrase	Definition	Sentence about Text
used to (pg. 14)	happened in the past but does not happen now	Henry **used to** walk to school by himself.
alone (pg. 14)	without anyone that you know	He used to walk to school **alone**.
worry (pg. 14)	to be concerned or nervous	Before Mudge, Henry used to **worry** when he walked to school.
tornadoes (pg. 14)	dangerous, swirling wind and rain storms	Henry was afraid of **tornadoes**.
ghosts (pg. 14)	shadowy figures of people	Henry worried about **ghosts** on his way to school.
bullies (pg. 14)	people who pick on others	Henry worried about **bullies** bothering him on his way to school.
straight ahead (pg. 15)	right in your path; in a direct line	Henry looked **straight ahead**.
never (pg. 15)	not ever; not at any time	Henry **never** looked back.
thought about (pg. 16)	to imagine or visualize in the mind	Henry **thought about** good dreams.
backward (pg. 16)	in reverse	Now, when Henry walks to school with Mudge, sometimes he walks **backward**.

© Shell Education

Pages 14–17

Name _____ Date _____

Vocabulary Activity

Directions: Draw lines to match the sentences.

Beginnings of Sentences	Endings of Sentences
Henry used to	looks back.
Henry **never**	to school **backward**.
He is afraid of	he gets Mudge.
Henry doesn't **worry** after	walk to school **alone**.
Sometimes Henry walks	**ghosts, bullies**, and **tornadoes**.

Directions: Answer this question.

1. Describe what Henry **thinks about** when he walks to school with Mudge.

_____

_____

Teacher Plans—Section 2

Henry Walks to School (pages 14–17)
Analyzing the Literature

Provided below are discussion questions you can use in small groups, with the whole class, or for written assignments. Each question is written at two levels so you can choose the right question for each group of students. For each question, a few key points are provided for your reference as you discuss the book with students.

Story Element	Level 1	Level 2	Key Discussion Points
Plot	Why doesn't Henry worry anymore on his way to school?	How do Henry's thoughts change when Mudge is with him?	Henry is afraid to walk to school alone. He worries about real and not-so-real dangers that could happen to him. When Mudge is with him, he isn't afraid of anything, and so his thoughts change to the things that he loves and things that make him happy.
Character	What is Henry afraid of?	Which of Henry's fears are real and which are probably not likely to happen?	Henry is afraid of tornadoes, ghosts, biting dogs, and bullies. Henry probably is not going to experience a tornado or a ghost, but he might have bad experiences with biting dogs and bullies.
Plot	Why does walking to school with Mudge make Henry happy?	Why do you think Henry thinks happy thoughts and does silly things after Mudge starts walking him to school?	Henry probably feels much more secure walking with a big dog. He probably knows that Mudge will protect him from anything, so he is free to relax and have fun.

© Shell Education — #40106—Instructional Guide: Henry and Mudge: The First Book

Reader Response

Think

Think about something that you used to be afraid of but doesn't scare you anymore.

Narrative Writing Prompt

Write about something you used to be scared of, but now you are not. Explain how you changed so you are not afraid anymore.

_____
_____
_____
_____
_____
_____
_____
_____
_____
_____

Name _____ Date _____

Pages 14-17

Guided Close Reading

Closely reread about Henry's walks to school before and after he gets Mudge (pages 14–17).

Directions: Think about these questions. In the space below, write ideas or draw pictures as you think. Be ready to share your answers.

❶ What word in the story means *concerned* or *afraid*?

❷ Which sentence shows that Henry wants to get to school in a hurry?

❸ What text shows that Henry is more comfortable walking to school with Mudge?

Pages 14-17

Name _____ Date _____

Making Connections–Worried or Not?

Directions: What kinds of things make you feel worried? What kinds of things make you feel safe? Write the items from the Word Bank in at least one column. Then, add a few more ideas under each column.

Word Bank

dogs	family	tornadoes	my home
bullies	spooky noises	good friends	strangers

Makes Me Worry	Makes Me Feel Safe

Name _____ Date _____

Pages 14-17

Language Learning

Directions: The words on this page are all found in this section of the story. These words are all spelled wrong. Check the spelling and rewrite the misspelled words. At the bottom of the page, write a sentence about the story using at least two of the words.

Language Hints!

- It's a good idea to use a dictionary to check the spelling of words.
- Don't forget to use the guide words at the top of each page in a dictionary.

schol   _____

abot   _____

dogz   _____

looced   _____

wiht   _____

hapy   _____

_____
_____
_____
_____

Pages 14–17

Name _____ Date _____

Story Elements–Character

Directions: Henry is afraid to walk to school alone. Draw pictures of two things that make you afraid when you are alone. Describe your pictures.

_____

_____

_____

_____

Name _____ Date _____

Pages 14-17

Story Elements-Setting

Directions: Write a detailed description of the path Henry takes as he walks to school. Include the places where scary things could hide.

Teacher Plans—Section 3

Mudge in Henry's Room (pages 18–22)

Vocabulary Overview

Key words and phrases from this section are provided below with definitions and sentences about how the words are used in the story. Introduce and discuss these important vocabulary words with students. If you think these words or other words in the story warrant more time devoted to them, there are suggestions in the introduction for other vocabulary activities (page 5).

Word	Definition	Sentence about Text
loved (pg. 18)	cared for deeply	Mudge **loves** the things in Henry's room.
dirty (pg. 18)	not clean	Mudge loves the **dirty** socks.
stuffed bear (pg. 18)	a toy in the shape of a bear that is filled with soft material	Mudge loves the **stuffed bear**.
mostly (pg. 18)	describes a usual situation or condition	He **mostly** loves Henry's bed.
climb (pg. 20)	to move or go up using your feet	Mudge likes to **climb** up on top of Henry's bed.
smells (pg. 20)	to use your nose to sense smells or odors	He **smells** Henry when they lie in bed.
milky (pg. 21)	looking, smelling, or tasting like milk	Mudge smells Henry's **milky** mouth.
soapy (pg. 21)	smelling like soap	Mudge smells Henry's **soapy** ears.
looked (pg. 22)	gazed or used one's vision	Mudge **looks** at things in Henry's room.
fell asleep (pg. 22)	changes from a waking state to a sleeping state	Mudge **falls asleep** by Henry.

Name _____ Date _____

Pages 18-22

Vocabulary Activity

Directions: Each of these sentences is from the story. Cut apart these sentence strips. Put the sentences in order based on the events in the story.

"And he **fell asleep**."

"But **mostly** he **loved** Henry's bed."

"He smelled his **soapy** ears."

"Mudge **loved** Henry's room."

"Then he **loved** to smell him."

"He **looked** at the bear."

Teacher Plans—Section 3

Mudge in Henry's Room (pages 18–22)

Analyzing the Literature

Provided below are discussion questions you can use in small groups, with the whole class, or for written assignments. Each question is written at two levels so you can choose the right question for each group of students. For each question, a few key points are provided for your reference as you discuss the book with students.

Story Element	Level 1	Level 2	Key Discussion Points
Setting	What does Mudge love most in Henry's room?	Why does Mudge love Henry's bed?	There are many things in Henry's room that are interesting to Mudge, but he loves Henry's bed the most. Henry's smell is on the bed and often Henry is in the bed, and Mudge likes to be near Henry.
Plot	Why do you think Mudge wants to sleep in Henry's bed?	Where is Mudge's favorite place to be and why?	Mudge's favorite place is Henry's bed because Henry is often in it. It probably smells like Henry even when Henry isn't there.
Character	What are some of the things Mudge loves in Henry's room?	Why would Mudge like Henry's dirty socks?	Mudge loves the dirty socks, stuffed bear, the fish tank, and the bed. The socks probably smell like Henry, and Mudge wants to feel close to him.

Name _____ Date _____

Pages 18–22

Reader Response

Think

Think about different things that you like to smell.

Opinion Writing Prompt

What things smell the best in the whole world? Be sure to include specific reasons why you enjoy smelling each item.

_____
_____
_____
_____
_____
_____
_____
_____
_____

Pages 18-22

Name _____ Date _____

Guided Close Reading

Closely reread about how Mudge loves Henry's room (pages 18–21).

Directions: Think about these questions. In the space below, write ideas or draw pictures as you think. Be ready to share your answers.

❶ What adjectives are included in this section?

❷ Based on the text, what is Mudge's favorite thing in Henry's room?

❸ What evidence in the text shows that Mudge loves Henry?

Name _____ Date _____

Pages 18-22

Making Connections–My Bedroom

Directions: Think about all the things in your bedroom. Which things are your favorites? Which things would a dog love best? Draw a map of your bedroom. Circle in red the things you love best. Circle in blue the things a dog would love best. Use symbols to represent the furniture, the doors, and the windows. Include a key for your map to explain your symbols.

Pages 18–22

Name _____ Date _____

Language Learning–Root Words

Directions: The words below are from this section of the book. Each of these words has a suffix added to the root word. Write each root word and each suffix below. The first one is done for you.

Language Hints!

- A suffix is an ending added to a word.
- The root word is a word with no suffixes or prefixes.

Word	Root Word	Suffix
1. loved	love	-ed
2. stuffed		
3. mostly		
4. smelled		
5. milky		
6. soapy		
7. looked		
8. licked		

Directions: Write a sentence about the story using at least three of the words from above.

_____

_____

Name _____ Date _____

Pages 18–22

Story Elements–Character

Directions: List at least 10 different things Mudge might do when Henry is away at school.

1. _____
2. _____
3. _____
4. _____
5. _____
6. _____
7. _____
8. _____
9. _____
10. _____

Pages 18-22

Name _____ Date _____

Story Elements–Setting

Directions: Fill in the Venn diagram below to compare and contrast your bedroom to Henry's bedroom. Include at least four items in each section of the Venn diagram.

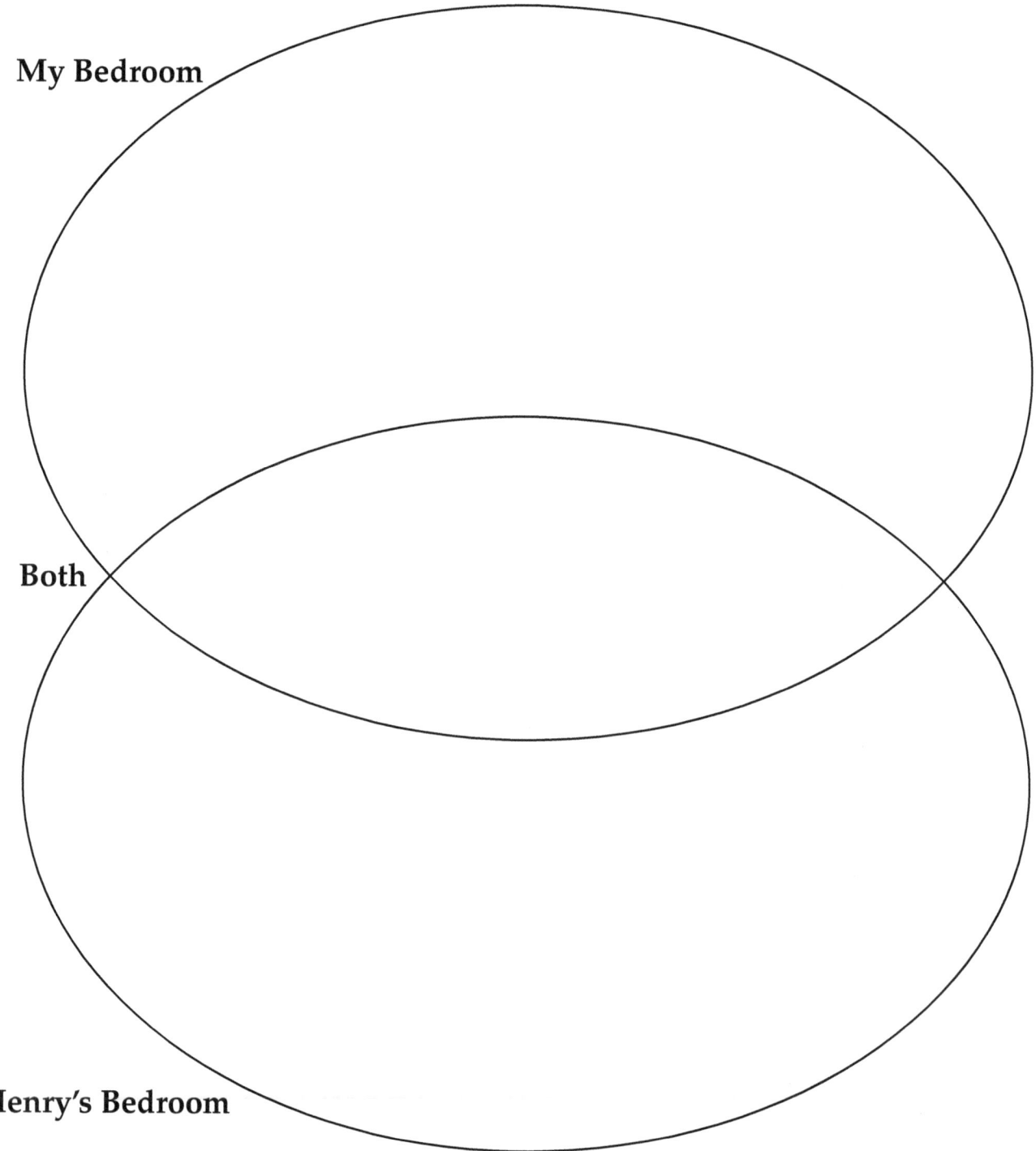

Teacher Plans—Section 4

Mudge Gets Lost (pages 23-34)
Vocabulary Overview

Key words and phrases from this section are provided below with definitions and sentences about how the words are used in the story. Introduce and discuss these important vocabulary words with students. If you think these words or other words in the story warrant more time devoted to them, there are suggestions in the introduction for other vocabulary activities (page 5).

Word	Definition	Sentence about Text
shining (pg. 23)	bright; shimmering	The sun is **shining**.
couldn't (pg. 23)	contraction for *could not*	Mudge **couldn't** find his way home.
sniffing (pg. 24)	using the nose to smell	Mudge is **sniffing** the ground.
bushes (pg. 24)	plants that have stems of wood and are smaller than a tree	Mudge is sniffing the **bushes**.
stream (pg. 24)	a small river	A **stream** runs through the woods.
porch (pg. 26)	a structure attached to the entrance of a building that has a roof and that may or may not have walls	Mudge cannot smell his front **porch**.
whined (pg. 27)	cried	Mudge **whines** for Henry.
hour (pg. 29)	60 minutes	Henry cries for an **hour**.
called (pg. 30)	shouted out	Henry **calls** for Mudge to come home.
lonely (pg. 34)	feeling sad and alone	Mudge is **lonely** without Henry.

Pages 23–34

Name _____ Date _____

Vocabulary Activity

Directions: Complete each sentence below with one of the vocabulary words listed here.

Words from the Story

couldn't	shining	sniffing	whines	calls
stream	lonely	bushes	porch	hour

1. The sun is _____ in the sky.

2. By himself, Mudge feels _____.

3. Mudge _____ find his way home.

4. Mudge is sad, and he sits down and _____.

Directions: Answer this question.

5. What does Henry do when Mudge gets lost?

_____

_____

_____

_____

Teacher Plans—Section 4

Mudge Gets Lost (pages 23-34)

Analyzing the Literature

Provided below are discussion questions you can use in small groups, with the whole class, or for written assignments. Each question is written at two levels so you can choose the right question for each group of students. For each question, a few key points are provided for your reference as you discuss the book with students.

Story Element	Level 1	Level 2	Key Discussion Points
Plot	Why do you think Mudge leaves home?	How does Henry know Mudge would never run away?	Mudge is probably curious about the world and wants to explore. He does not think he will get lost. Henry knows how much Mudge loves him and that he would never leave him on purpose, so he figures Mudge must be lost.
Character	What does Mudge do when he realizes he is lost?	How do you think Mudge feels when he cannot find his way home?	Mudge looks around and he sniffs. Then, he just lays down on the ground. He probably feels sad, lonely, and worried.
Plot	What does Henry do when he first realizes Mudge is gone?	What makes Henry realize that Mudge must be lost?	Henry calls for him and then he cries. Then, Henry realizes that Mudge would never leave him on purpose, so he must be lost.
Plot	What does Henry do to find Mudge?	Why do you think Henry calls out Mudge's name?	Henry looks for Mudge. He looks down the road, in a field, and in the trees. Henry calls out because he thinks maybe Mudge will hear him.

© Shell Education #40106—Instructional Guide: Henry and Mudge: The First Book

Pages 23-34

Name _____ Date _____

Reader Response

Think

Mudge becomes lost from Henry in this part of the story. Think about what you should do if you ever become lost.

Informative/Explanatory Writing Prompt

Write the steps you should take if you ever get lost. List several ideas of what you could do to help find your way.

_____
_____
_____
_____
_____
_____
_____
_____
_____
_____
_____
_____

Name _____ Date _____

Pages 23-34

Guided Close Reading

Closely reread about Mudge getting lost (pages 24–27).

Directions: Think about these questions. In the space below, write ideas or draw pictures as you think. Be ready to share your answers.

❶ Which words in the story show that Mudge traveled a long way from home?

❷ Use the text to show that Mudge was not paying attention to where he was going.

❸ What text helps you understand that Mudge knows he is lost?

© Shell Education　　#40106—Instructional Guide: Henry and Mudge: The First Book　　45

Pages 23-34

Name _____ Date _____

Making Connections—Alphabetical Order

Directions: Think of a time when you were sad. What words describe your feelings? When Mudge is lost, both he and Henry have sad feelings. Rewrite the sad words below in alphabetical order. Then, write at least five words for happy feelings. Put those in alphabetical order, as well.

Words from the Section	Alphabetize
hurt	_____
whined	_____
crying	_____
alone	_____
lonely	_____

Words for Happy Feelings

1. _____

2. _____

3. _____

4. _____

5. _____

Name _____   Date _____

Pages 23-34

Language Learning–Blending Sounds

Directions: Some of the words from the story begin with consonant blends. Add a blend to each word ending below to make a word from this section of the book. Use the book to make sure you have made the right words! Write the whole words in the boxes.

Language Hints!

- A blend is when 2 or 3 different consonant sounds are together.
- Each blend sound is clearly heard.

Word Bank

tr–	fl–	str–	fr–
sn–	cr–	sm–	sw–

____ -ell

____ -eet

____ -ying

____ -ont

____ -ied

____ -ees

____ -eam

____ -iffing

© Shell Education   #40106—Instructional Guide: Henry and Mudge: The First Book

Pages 23-34

Name _____ Date _____

Story Elements–Plot

Directions: The plot of a story is made up of events. Number the events below in the order they happen in the book. At the bottom of the page, describe your favorite part of this section of the book.

_____ Mudge runs to Henry.

_____ Henry is sad.

_____ Mudge goes through a field.

_____ Mudge takes a walk.

_____ Mudge is lost.

_____ Henry looks for Mudge.

_____
_____
_____
_____
_____
_____
_____
_____

Name _____ Date _____

Pages 23-34

Story Elements–Setting

Directions: Mudge walks down a road, through a field, across a stream, and into pine trees. Draw pictures of the places Mudge went.

down a road	through a field
across a stream	into pine trees

© Shell Education · #40106—*Instructional Guide: Henry and Mudge: The First Book* · 49

Teacher Plans—Section 5

Henry and Mudge Back Together (pages 35-40)

Vocabulary Overview

Key words and phrases from this section are provided below with definitions and sentences about how the words are used in the story. Introduce and discuss these important vocabulary words with students. If you think these words or other words in the story warrant more time devoted to them, there are suggestions in the introduction for other vocabulary activities (page 5).

Word	Definition	Sentence about Text
woke up (pg. 35)	stopped sleeping; became awake after sleeping	When Henry **wakes up**, he sees Mudge's head.
breakfast (pg. 36)	a morning meal	Henry and Mudge eat **breakfast** together.
supper (pg. 36)	dinner; an evening meal	Henry and Mudge eat **supper** together.
waited (pg. 37)	stayed in a place until someone arrived	Mudge **waits** for Henry.
worried (pg. 37)	concerned	Henry never **worries** about his dog.
silent (pg. 39)	quiet; making no noise	The road is long and **silent**.
wide (pg. 39)	extending a great distance from one side to the other; not narrow	Henry sees big, **wide** fields in his dream.
remembered (pg. 39)	recalled; opposite of forgot	Mudge **remembers** his dream.
closer (pg. 40)	near in place	Henry and Mudge stay **closer** to each other.
fear (pg. 40)	being afraid	Henry feels **fear** when he loses Mudge.

Name _____ Date _____

Pages 35-40

Vocabulary Activity

Directions: Practice your vocabulary and writing skills. Write at least three sentences using words from the story. Make sure your sentences show what the words mean.

Words from the Story

woke up	breakfast	supper	waited	worried
silent	wide	remembered	closer	fear

_____

_____

_____

_____

_____

_____

Directions: Answer this question.

1. What does Henry **remember** in his dream about **fear**?

_____

_____

Teacher Plans—Section 5

Henry and Mudge Back Together (pages 35–40)

Analyzing the Literature

Provided below are discussion questions you can use in small groups, with the whole class, or for written assignments. Each question is written at two levels so you can choose the right question for each group of students. For each question, a few key points are provided for your reference as you discuss the book with students.

Story Element	Level 1	Level 2	Key Discussion Points
Plot	What does Henry see when he wakes up every morning?	What does Mudge do every morning?	Henry sees Mudge's big head when he wakes up because Mudge looks into Henry's face to wait for him to wake up.
Plot	What things do Henry and Mudge do at the same time?	How can you tell that Henry and Mudge like to do things together?	They eat their meals together because they do not want to be away from each other.
Setting	What do Henry and Mudge see in their dreams?	How do you think the dreams make them feel?	They see a long road, streams, and pine trees. They are both alone in the dreams, so they probably do not like it. It might make them feel fearful.
Character	What are some words that describe Mudge?	How do you know that Mudge is a good friend to Henry?	Mudge is loyal and loving and protective. He always wants to be near Henry and spends all of his time with him.

Name _____ Date _____

Pages 35-40

Reader Response

Think

Think about a wonderful dream that you have had.

Narrative Writing Prompt

Describe a wonderful dream that you have had. Make sure to include details about your dream and why it was a good dream.

_____
_____
_____
_____
_____
_____
_____
_____
_____
_____
_____

Guided Close Reading

Closely reread about the dreams that Henry and Mudge have (pages 38–39).

Directions: Think about these questions. In the space below, write ideas or draw pictures as you think. Be ready to share your answers.

❶ What information does the picture give you about the characters?

❷ Use the text to describe Henry's dream and Mudge's dream.

❸ How can Henry tell that Mudge would never leave him again?

Name _____ Date _____

Making Connections–Shapes

Directions: After Mudge comes home, he and Henry eat together. Draw a picture of the two friends eating. In the picture, include at least three circles, three triangles, three squares, and three rectangles. For example, you could make a bowl that's a circle and a napkin that's a rectangle.

○ △ ▢ ▭

Pages 35-40

Name _____ Date _____

Language Learning–Nouns, Nouns, Nouns

Directions: Look at the words in the Word Bank below. These words are different kinds of nouns from the story. Put each word from the story in the correct category.

Language Hints!

- Common nouns name non-specific people, places, and things.
- Proper nouns name specific people, places, and things.
- Possessive nouns show that something belongs to someone.

Word Bank

Mudge's head	school	breakfast
Mudge	Henry	Henry's face

Common Nouns
_____
_____

Proper Nouns
_____
_____

Possessive Nouns
_____
_____

Name _____ Date _____

Pages 35-40

Story Elements-Plot

Directions: Stories often have happy endings. Describe how this story ends in a happy way. Draw a picture to go with your description.

_____
_____
_____
_____
_____
_____
_____

Pages 35-40

Name _____ Date _____

Story Elements-Setting

Directions: Mudge and Henry have scary dreams of being lost from each other. Draw a picture showing what is the same in their dreams.

Name _____ Date _____

Post-Reading Activities

Post-Reading Theme Thoughts

Directions: Pretend you are Henry or Mudge. Draw a picture of a happy face or a sad face to show how the character would feel about each statement. Then explain your answer.

Character I Chose: _____

Statement	How Does He Feel? 😊 ☹️	Explain Your Answer
Dogs make great friends.		
Being alone can be scary.		
It is sad to lose a pet.		
It is not important to have a close friend.		

Post-Reading Activities

Culminating Activity: Reader's Theater

Directions: Explain to students that a reader's theater is like a play. The major difference is that students can read their parts during the performance. Tell them that they will pair up. One person will be Henry, and the other person will be Mudge.

Masks

Duplicate the Henry and Mudge masks on pages 61–62. Have students cut out their masks. Use a hole puncher to punch holes through the small circles at the outer edges of each mask. Then, loop a small rubber band through each hole. These go around a child's ears to hold the mask in place. You can also tie the masks on with string or yarn.

Practicing Parts

Duplicate the reader's theater script on page 63. Help students identify their parts on the script. Model for them how to read with expression. Have students think about how Henry might speak to Mudge and how Mudge might sound when he talks. Allow students to practice reading their parts aloud numerous times before performing.

Culminating Activity: Reader's Theater (cont.)

Post-Reading Activities

Culminating Activity: Reader's Theater (cont.)

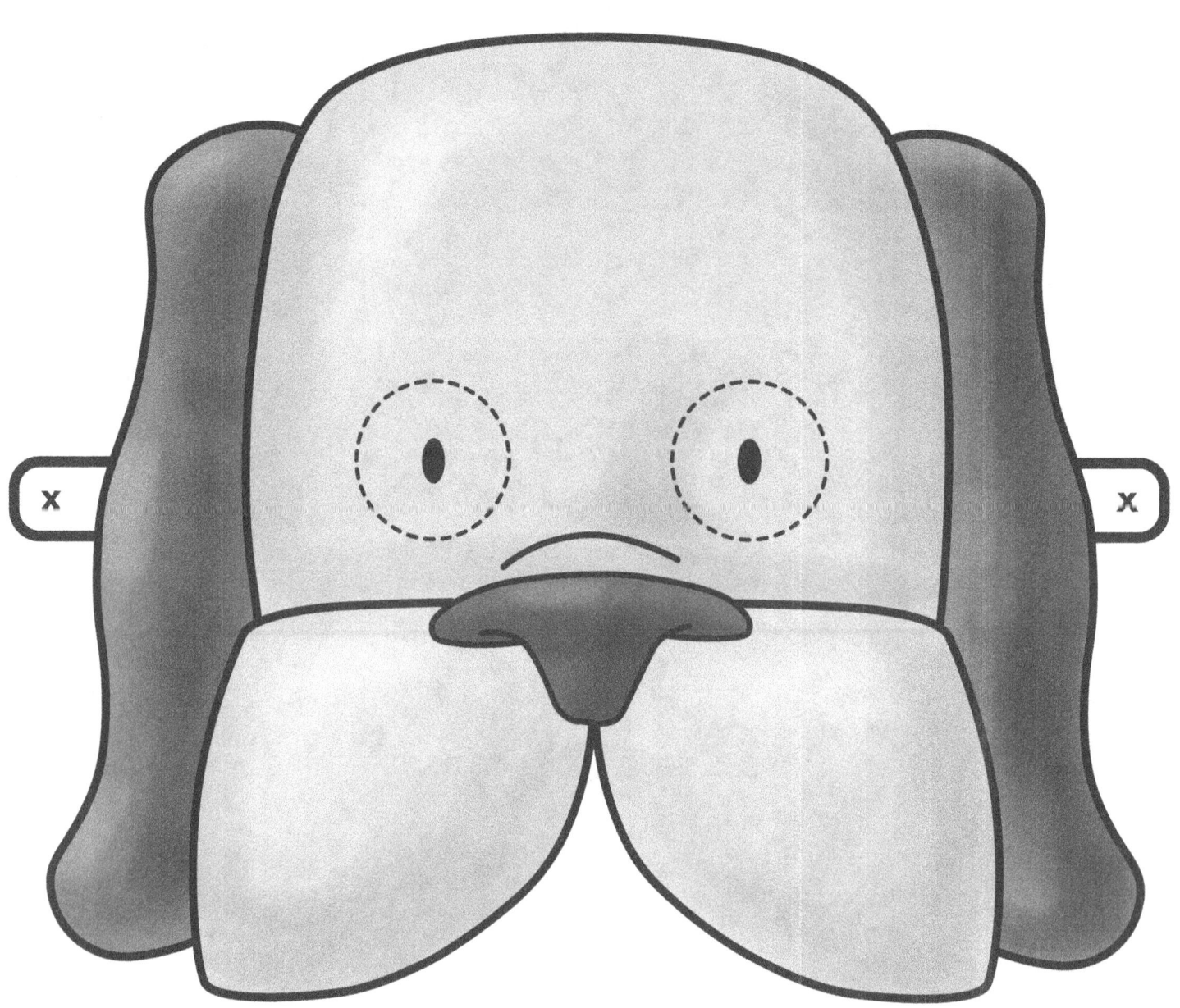

Culminating Activity: Reader's Theater (cont.)

Henry and Mudge: A Reader's Theater

Henry: I'm so glad you're my dog, Mudge!

Mudge: I love you, Henry!

Henry: Walking to school makes me worried. Will you walk with me?

Mudge: Sure, Henry! I can keep you safe.

Henry: See you after school, Mudge!

Mudge: I'll wait for you in your room.

After School

Henry: Hi, Mudge! What did you do today?

Mudge: I looked at all the cool things in your room, but I missed you.

Mudge Gets Lost

Henry: Mudge! Mudge! Where are you? Oh, Mudge, I'm so sad without you.

Mudge: I'm so lonely. I don't know how to find my way home.

Henry: Mudge! Mudge! Can you hear me?

Mudge: Henry, I'm here! I was lost.

Henry: You're a great dog, Mudge. Don't ever leave me again.

Mudge: I would be afraid to leave you, Henry. I like being with you.

Henry: You're the best dog and my very best friend.

Mudge: You are my best friend, too, Henry.

Post-Reading Activities

Name _____ Date _____

Comprehension Assessment

Directions: Fill in the best response to each question.

Section 1—Henry Gets a Dog

1. What shows that Henry is happy he is going to get a dog?

   (A) "Henry searched for a dog."

   (B) "I want a brother."

   (C) "I want to hug you!"

   (D) "Then he found Mudge."

Section 2—Henry Walks to School

2. Why does Henry walk to school quickly?

   (E) He is afraid to walk alone.

   (F) He does not like school.

   (G) He does not feel good.

   (H) He is late.

Section 3—Mudge in Henry's Room

3. What shows that Mudge likes Henry's bed the most?

   (A) The bed is colorful.

   (B) He hides under the bed when Henry is gone.

   (C) The fish tank is near the bed.

   (D) He climbs in bed with Henry.

Comprehension Assessment (cont.)

Section 4—Mudge Gets Lost

4. Describe the difference in how Mudge feels from when he starts on his walk to when he gets lost.

_____

_____

_____

_____

_____

_____

Section 5—Henry and Mudge Back Together

5. What shows that Henry is happy to have Mudge with him again?

- (E) He eats breakfast.
- (F) He stays close to Mudge.
- (G) Mudge does not leave home.
- (H) Henry has dreams.

Post-Reading Activities

Name _____ Date _____

Response to Literature: Benefits of Owning a Pet

Directions: Owning a pet is fun. It is also a big responsibility. Pets need love and care. Sometimes, owning a pet can be scary or sad if a pet gets old or sick. Most pet owners believe the good times outweigh the bad times. Complete the word web below with reasons that owning a pet is worth it. Then, answer the questions on the next page.

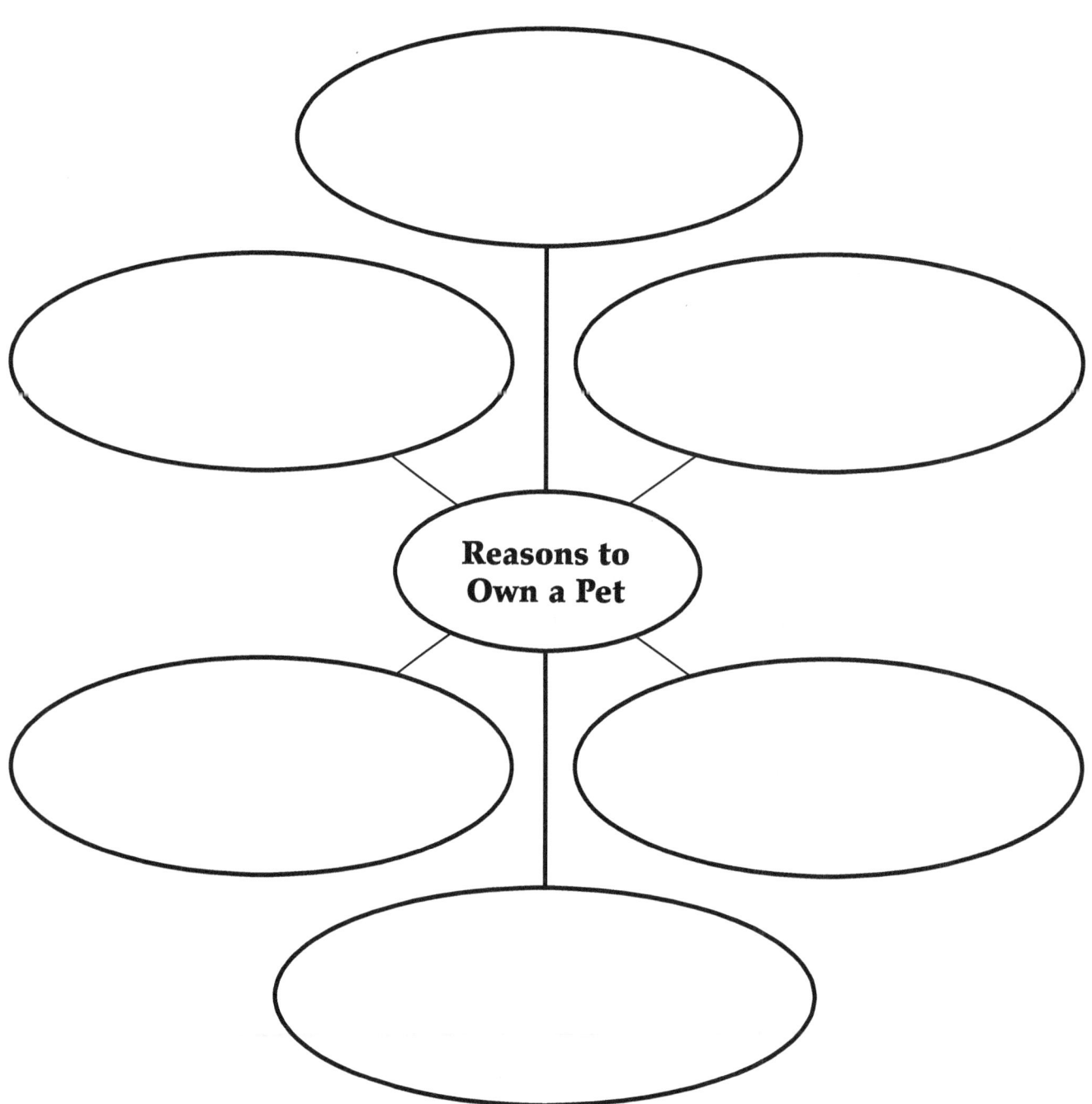

Name _____ Date _____

Response to Literature: Benefits of Owning a Pet (cont.)

1. What is the best reason for having a pet?

   _____
   _____
   _____
   _____

2. How do pets improve our lives?

   _____
   _____
   _____
   _____

3. What do you think Henry loves most about Mudge?

   _____
   _____
   _____
   _____

Post-Reading Activities

Name _____ Date _____

Response to Literature Rubric

Directions: Use this rubric to evaluate student responses.

Great Job	Good Work	Keep Trying
☐ You answered all three questions completely. You included many details.	☐ You answered all three questions.	☐ You did not answer all three questions.
☐ Your handwriting is very neat. There are no spelling errors.	☐ Your handwriting can be neater. There are some spelling errors.	☐ Your handwriting is not very neat. There are many spelling errors.
☐ Your picture is neat and fully colored.	☐ Your picture is neat and some of it is colored.	☐ Your picture is not very neat and/or fully colored.
☐ Creativity is clear in both the picture and the writing.	☐ Creativity is clear in either the picture or the writing.	☐ There is not much creativity in either the picture or the writing.

Teacher Comments: _____

_____

_____

Writing Paper 1

Name _____ Date _____

_____

Writing Paper 2

Name _____ Date _____

Answer Key

The responses provided here are just examples of what students may answer. Many accurate responses are possible for the questions throughout this unit.

Vocabulary Activity—Section 1:
Henry Gets a Dog (page 15)

1. A dog can play. A dog spends time with you. A dog loves you.

Guided Close Reading—Section 1:
Henry Gets a Dog (page 18)

1. He is a puppy.
2. Mudge licks Henry and lies on Henry.
3. Henry says he wants to hug his parents.

Making Connections—Section 1:
Henry Gets a Dog (page 19)

Dog	Cat
food	food
toys	toys
water	water
love	love
leash	litter box

Language Learning—Section 1:
Henry Gets a Dog (page 20)

The following two-syllable words should be circled: brother, parents, Henry, sorry, collars, almost, because, children, okay, curly, pointed, floppy, puppy, growing, and seven.

Vocabulary Activity—Section 2:
Henry Walks to School (page 24)

- Henry used to walk to school **alone**.
- Henry **never** looks back.
- He is afraid of **ghosts**, **bullies**, and **tornadoes**.
- Henry doesn't **worry** after he gets Mudge.
- Sometimes Henry walks to school **backward**.

1. Henry thinks about vanilla ice cream, rain, rocks, and good dreams.

Guided Close Reading—Section 2:
Henry Walks to School (page 27)

1. worried
2. He walks as fast as he can.
3. He thinks about happy things like ice cream, rain, rocks, and good dreams. He does not walk fast. Sometimes, he walks backward.

Making Connections—Section 2:
Henry Walks to School (page 28)

Makes Me Worry	Makes Me Feel Safe
tornadoes	family
bullies	my home
spooky noises	good friends
strangers	

dogs *(can be in either column)*

Story Elements—Section 2:
Henry Walks to School (page 29)

The corrected spelling is as follows: school, about, dogs, looked, with, and happy. Students should also write a sentence using at least two of the words.

Vocabulary Activity—Section 3:
Mudge in Henry's Room (page 33)

- "Mudge **loved** Henry's room."
- "But **mostly** he **loved** Henry's bed."
- "Then he **loved** to smell him."
- "He smelled his **soapy** ears."
- "He **looked** at the bear."
- "And he **fell asleep**."

Guided Close Reading—Section 3:
Mudge in Henry's Room (page 36)

1. The adjectives include: dirty, stuffed, fish, and Henry's.
2. His favorite thing is Henry's bed.
3. Mudge sleeps on Henry's bed, and Mudge sniffs and licks Henry.

Language Learning—Section 3:
Mudge in Henry's Room (page 38)

1. loved	love	-ed
2. stuffed	stuff	-ed
3. mostly	most	-ly
4. smelled	smell	-ed
5. milky	milk	-y
6. soapy	soap	-y
7. looked	look	-ed
8. licked	lick	-ed

Answer Key

Vocabulary Activity—Section 4:
Mudge Gets Lost (page 42)

1. The sun is **shining** in the sky.
2. By himself, Mudge feels **lonely**.
3. Mudge **couldn't** find his way home.
4. Mudge is sad, and he sits down and **whines**.
5. Henry cries, and then he goes to look for Mudge.

Guided Close Reading—Section 4:
Mudge Gets Lost (page 45)

1. He goes down the road, through a field, across a stream, into pine trees, and out to the other side.
2. He sniffs bushes and kicks up dust.
3. He cries and his heart hurts.

Making Connections—Section 4:
Mudge Gets Lost (page 46)

The alphabetical list is: alone, crying, hurt, lonely, and whines. Students should also include at least five words for happy feelings.

Language Learning—Section 4:
Mudge Gets Lost (page 47)

Although other words can be formed, this list shows where the specific words are in the book.

- smell (page 26)
- sweet (page 23); street (page 26)
- flying (page 23); crying (page 29)
- front (page 26)
- cried (page 29)
- trees (page 24)
- stream (pages 24, 32)
- sniffing (page 24)

Story Elements—Section 4:
Mudge Gets Lost (page 48)

6 Mudge runs to Henry.
4 Henry is sad.
2 Mudge goes through a field.
1 Mudge takes a walk.
3 Mudge is lost.
5 Henry looks for Mudge.

Vocabulary Activity—Section 5:
Henry and Mudge Back Together (page 51)

1. He remembers that he and Mudge were not together.

Guided Close Reading—Section 5:
Henry and Mudge Back Together (page 54)

1. Mudge stays at home and waits for Henry.
2. They dream of long roads, fields, streams, pine trees, and being alone.
3. Mudge stays with Henry all the time.

Language Learning—Section 5:
Henry and Mudge Back Together (page 56)

Common Noun	Proper Noun	Possesive Noun
school	Mudge	Mudge's head
breakfast	Henry	Henry's face

Comprehension Assessment (pages 64–65)

1. C. "I want to hug you!"
2. E. He is afraid to walk alone.
3. D. He climbs in bed with Henry.
4. Mudge is busy and interested in everything. He runs and sniffs. Then when he is lost, he is sad so he lies down and whines.
5. F. He stays close to Mudge.